CONTENTS

BLOCK 3
ENGLISH IN USE

Diana Honeybone

INTRODUCTION

The first course book and its associated study materials have introduced two important aspects of English: the changes that took place in its history and the structure of present-day English. Block 3 takes us on to consider some of the many functions of English in daily life and the uses to which it is put in order to achieve particular aims. It moves the focus from the description of the structure of English to examining its functions in action in a range of specific contexts.

Week 10 looks at the use of English in everyday conversations. We examine how it is used for establishing social relationships as well as for passing on ideas and information. We study in detail the structures and techniques that are used to manage and take part in daily conversation.

Week 11 moves on to the varieties of literacy practice that govern the everyday reading and writing of English, and shows how these are related to the contexts within which English is used.

In week 12, we focus on a specific area of daily use of English: the language used at work. How far does this differ from the everyday conversational English examined in week 10? What special features does it need to enable us to achieve set tasks in a work situation?

Week 13 concentrates on another significant area of specific use of English: the language of persuasion. We investigate how far the language we use to persuade others to share our views has features in common with the speeches of the professional persuaders such as politicians and evangelists.

THEMES

The block carries forward some of the themes that you have already met in Blocks 1 and 2. These are summarized below where we also point out how they relate to the study material in this block. It would be useful to check on them now so that you are aware of them as you work through the material. Then come back to them as a focus for your thoughts when you review the block. The individual study questions for each week will be given at the beginning of the notes for that week; they will help you in looking out for the themes.

English in context — Block 2 demonstrated how variations in the speech of individuals are a response to different situations. Block 3 takes this further, showing the significance of context in our use and understanding of specific forms of English. Chapter 1 of the course book is helpful in defining 'context'.

Varieties of English — This block considers variation in English in two ways. First, we extend our study of social, regional and cultural variation.

Secondly, we look at variation in a wider sense, examining the variety of language practices, discourses and texts that relate to the demands of work and social situations in everyday life.

Changing English The theme of changing practices and structures in English is a necessary part of this block, since it is concerned with the changing contexts of daily life, which are reflected in the forms of English that they generate.

Achieving things in English This is an important theme in Block 3 as it is concerned with the language in action, being put to practical uses. We study English as a spoken and written means of creating and maintaining social relationships, organizing work and persuading people to support a political or religious belief.

English and identity The concern with English as a means of creating and maintaining identity is also a feature of Block 3. Personal identity in social and workplace relationships, gender and nationality are all considered in relation to language use.

As you study Block 3, you will be aware that the emphasis of the course material, and the perspectives from which it is approached, are different in some ways from those of Block 2. Week 8, with its concentration on context, pointed the way towards this change of emphasis. While we shall still be concentrating on many of the same themes that you have met in the course so far, in Block 3 we shall be giving particular attention to English in its social and cultural context. We shall also ask you to think about the related topic of the functions that English serves. You will be considering the ways in which language is used in work and social situations, for specific purposes, and the effects of this in creating groups of users, drawn together by their use of the language in particular ways to achieve a common goal.

The model of English that we shall use draws on the ideas of the linguist Michael Halliday; these underpin much of the discussion in the study material of Block 3. Look out for the reference to his work in Chapter 1 of the second course book (week 10). In week 11, you will have an opportunity to investigate Halliday's ideas in more depth, and to see how they relate to the later chapters of this block. You may find it interesting to compare Halliday's approach to language with the ideas of other linguists whom you come across as you study this course.

STUDYING BLOCK 3

Block 3 occupies four weeks of study (weeks 10–13). It contains the following components:

- course book *Using English: from conversation to canon*, Chapters 1–4
- set book *Describing Language*, sections of Chapters 1, 3, 6 and 7
- Audiocassette 3 Bands 1–9
- Video Bands 2 and 3
- TV 3 'English Only' in America
- TMA 03 Options (a) and (b)

There are also practical activities, many of which are related to the audio and video cassettes. In this block, for instance, you will learn how to make a transcript of English conversations and other extended sequences of talk, and you will also learn different ways of analysing spoken and written language. The notes in this guide provide support with such analysis. As in previous blocks you are encouraged to relate material in the course to your own experience, and to approach materials critically. We recommend that you keep a 'cuttings file' of material relevant to Block 3; you can also add to your collection for Blocks 1 and 2, if you come across any appropriate material.

'English in use' file

Material that relates to Block 3 could include any extracts from newspapers or magazines that give interesting examples of daily conversation. You could note down any dialogue from radio or TV interviews, or from conversation that you overhear in daily life. Work-related jargon is also a feature of this block; look out for written examples of this in connection with your own or other people's work, or note down jargon that you hear. Public speaking is our final topic; any accounts of speeches as reported in the press or short extracts heard on TV or radio would be good material to collect for this. The study notes for week 11 will suggest some examples of everyday writing that you could add to your file. You may also find material related to past and future topics of the course.

The chart below gives suggested timings for each week (the notes for each week give more detailed timings for each component). Remember that these timings can only be approximate. You will complete some components more quickly than this, while others may take more time.

Week 10 contains a lot of new material and also includes practical activities. It is therefore a little heavy, but week 11 is much lighter to give you space to catch up if need be. As in earlier blocks, we have given a separate time allowance for the TMA to allow you some flexibility in planning your work. We do suggest, however, that you spread your work on the TMA over more than one week, and particularly that you carry out some substantive work on the assignment (selecting material, planning your answer) during week 12.

Study hint: before beginning work on the block you should look at the questions and notes for TMA 03 Options (a) and (b) so that, as you study, you can assemble material to answer your preferred option.

Study material	*Hours*
Week 10	13–14
Week 11	9–10
Week 12	$9\frac{1}{2}$–$10\frac{1}{2}$
Week 13	$8\frac{1}{2}$–$9\frac{1}{2}$
Block review and TMA 03 Options (a) and (b)	8
Total	48–52

WEEK 10 EVERYDAY TALK

Study questions

These are the main questions addressed in week 10. Bear them in mind as you study the material, and use them as a guide to summarizing what you have learned at the end of the study week. They are followed by notes to help you as you work through the readings and cassette bands.

Questions	**Related block themes**
What are the functions of everyday conversation?	*Achieving things in English*
How do social and cultural context and gender influence the style of everyday speech?	*English in context/English and identity/varieties of English*
What devices do we use to manage everyday conversation?	*Varieties of English*
How is narrative used in everyday situations to enable speakers to explore a range of identities?	*English and identity*

Introductory study notes and study chart

These are the components that you will need to work through this study week. They are listed in the order in which they should be studied.

Study chart for course week 10

Course book		*Set book*		
Chapter/teaching text	*Readings*	Describing Language	*Audiocassette 3*	*TV*
				TV 3 'English Only' in America
		6.3 Conversation management and 7.3 Spoken language		
1 Everyday talk	A Communicative strategies in Aboriginal English		Band 1 Introduction Band 2 Aboriginal English	
	B The role of compliments in female–male interaction		Band 3 Hedges and tag questions	
			Band 4 Aboriginal data	
Review of week 10: activity related to *Describing Language*, Chapter 6, section 6.4, and Audiocassette 3 Band 5 Informal talk				
Overview of your work				

This week's work introduces the block's main topic of 'English in action'. The specific form of English to be investigated in this study week is everyday conversation: its function in establishing and maintaining social relationships as well as conveying information; its grammatical structure and the contexts that can influence the form that it takes; the ways in which people use conversation to explore a range of identities and to achieve social cohesion. We shall also be aware of the changes that take place in conversational behaviour as the circumstances and audience change.

Most of the components of this week's study are closely interrelated. Probably the best way to work through them is to integrate listening to the audiocassette tapes with your reading of Chapter 1 of the course book, the extracts from *Describing Language*, and the viewing of TV 3, as explained in these notes. The extracts from *Describing Language* and the audiovisual material will help to illuminate the concepts discussed in the course book chapter and provide very helpful examples of talk to let you hear the features that you have been reading about.

This is rather a busy week, with the introduction of new concepts and with a number of cassette bands to listen to; but the workload is lighter in the remaining study weeks, you'll be pleased to know. You should have time to start thinking about TMA 03 by week 12.

The notes below take you through the components of the week's study in the order in which they appear above.

TV 3 'English Only' in America

(Allow about 1 hour)

> We recommend that, if possible, you video-record TV 3 so that you can review extracts in later weeks.

This programme connects with several of the topics studied in Block 3. It discusses the current attempts by pressure groups in some states of the USA to introduce a policy of using English, and only English, in organizations such as schools, factories and businesses. We are offered the arguments for and against such a policy and we consider the wider issues that are raised by this debate. The detailed notes that accompany this programme are at the end of this study guide, on p. 25. Please turn to the notes now, read them and watch the programme.

Describing Language Chapter 6, section 6.3 and Chapter 7, section 7.3

(Allow about 1 hour 30 minutes)

These sections discuss the structure of conversation and how this has been analysed. Section 6.3 discusses *conversation management* – the strategies people use to organize a conversation so that it (normally) flows smoothly. In section 7.3 it is the discussion of *conversation analysis* (pp. 200–219) that is particularly relevant to your work this week. These readings from *Describing Language* are related to section 1.2 in Chapter 1 of the course book, and you are advised to read them before starting the chapter. You will find that many terms and concepts explained in the readings from *Describing Language* are drawn on in the course book chapter.

As you read section 6.3, notice:

- the linguistic features which mark out transition-relevance places, such as turn-yielding cues by which the present speaker indicates that he or she is about to finish their speaking turn;
- what constitutes an interruption, and how participants in a conversation deal with it; also consider variation on the basic pattern of single-speaker turn taking, such as side-comments and duetting, and the contexts in which they occur.

In section 7.3, notice:

- the overall organization of conversation – e.g. how speakers draw conversations to a close; other examples of conversational sequences (requests, offers, questions, etc.). The notion of *adjacency pairs* (p. 204) is particularly important here;
- some problems associated with conversation analysis (pp. 207–9); you should bear in mind the issues discussed in relation to transcription and analysis when you come to try out your own transcription later this week.

Course book Chapter 1 Everyday talk

(*Allow 6–7 hours*)

This chapter helps to bring together the topics of this week. It introduces and explains the structure and functions of everyday conversation, illustrating these with a range of examples drawn from the worldwide use of English in its variant forms.

As you read this chapter, you will also be asked to pause and incorporate several other components of this week's work. As well as the reading from *Describing Language* referred to above, there are three bands from Audiocassette 3 which are particularly closely connected with the readings for Chapter 1. Please now look back to the study chart above to check on which bands go with which readings. There is more detailed guidance on this immediately following these notes on Chapter 1, and full notes on each band at the end of this guide.

While you study the chapter and its associated readings, bear in mind the change of emphasis from Block 2. We are still concerned with the structure of English, but in Blocks 3 and 4 we will relate this particularly to specific functions. Section 1.2 introduces you to the structure of everyday conversation; later, you will be able to compare this with more formal specialized styles.

The Introduction (section 1.1) defines the scope of the chapter and highlights the key issues. One issue that you should keep particularly in mind through this week's study is the cultural and linguistic background that people bring to their conversations. A shared background of implicit values, attitudes and assumptions is a vital ingredient in conversation; look out for examples of how its absence can cause misunderstandings and difficulties, especially between speakers from different cultures.

This chapter will help you to become aware of the amount of formal structure present, even in the most casual and apparently fragmented conversations. Look out for the formal features which distinguish different ways of using English. For example, the dialogic element – the references, whether implicit or explicit, to what others have said; the accepted framework for closing conversations, described for us in section 1.2; the skills of turn taking; in short, all the 'rules' that are applied in order to take part in daily conversation within our familiar social contexts. As you read through this, think back to your earlier reading from *Describing Language* (sections 6.3 and 7.3); ask yourself how far these 'rules' are found in the everyday dialogues that you take part in. Listen to the conversations around you. Can you detect these rules in action? Are you aware of 'face work' taking place? The chapter deals with rules for closing conversations – can you work out the appropriate rules for opening and closing everyday conversations in the different contexts that you meet?

Section 1.4 goes more deeply into the issue of context and its influence on conversational style. Be sure that you're clear about the meaning of *style* in relation to conversation; it is defined at the start of the section. Note how this differs from the meaning used in Block 2, especially week 8. The three examples demonstrate the range of variations in conversational style, but they cannot cover all of the possibilities within this range. As you study the examples, think about what aspects of the speakers' social backgrounds have influenced their style of conversation – factors such as geographical origin, culture and gender – and how these can lead to misunderstandings when they come into contact with the different practices of another culture. Diana Eades's reading and the interview with her on Audiocassette 3 throw light on this. You may wish to give some thought to the 'women's language' issue: how far is this specifically related to gender, or do other social or cultural factors play a part in determining when this style is used? Janet Holmes's reading and audiocassette band contain further helpful material on this issue.

The final section is concerned with the use of storytelling in everyday conversation as a way of affirming identity or trying out different identities. It links back to Block 2 in its discussion of codeswitching, and forward to Block 4 which will discuss narrative in its study of language as art.

Audiocassette 3 Band 1 Introduction and Band 2 Aboriginal English

(Allow about 30 minutes)

These bands go together with Reading A of Chapter 1. The first band introduces the cassette's themes and topics; there are no further notes in connection with it.

Band 2 is an interview with Diana Eades, the author of Reading A; she expands her discussion of Aboriginal English and its distinctive features. Detailed notes and an activity connected with this band are in the audiovisual notes at the end of this guide. Please turn now to these notes, read through them and listen to the cassette; then return to Chapter 1.

Audiocassette 3 Band 3 Hedges and tag questions

(Allow about 30 minutes)

This goes together with Reading B of Chapter 1. Janet Holmes, the author of the reading, explains her research and its significance more fully. There is also an activity connected with this band, which links with the work on Band 4. Please now turn to the detailed notes about this in the audiovisual notes at the end of this guide, and listen to this cassette. Then return to Chapter 1.

Audiocassette 3 Band 4 Aboriginal data

(*Allow about 1 hour*)

After you have finished reading Chapter 1 and listening to its associated bands, we move on to Band 4. This recorded conversation between two young Australian Aboriginal women links closely with the two previous bands. It gives you the opportunity to hear the features of language that Diana Eades and Janet Holmes have described, and to analyse this variety of English. Full notes on this band and the activity are at the end of this guide. Please turn to them now and work through the band.

Review of week 10

(*Allow about 2½ hours*)

This activity is designed to give you an opportunity to review the work of this study week, to consolidate it and to think about it for yourself. There are three parts to the review activity for this study week: a reading, an exercise in transcription and analysis connected with Band 5 of Audiocassette 3, and a look back over your work in this block so far.

Describing Language *Chapter 6, section 6.4*

(*Allow about 1 hour*)

This reading takes us on to the topic of how we observe and record conversation for further detailed study. As you read it, look for:

- the methods used to observe and record a conversation, both from live observation and by using audio and video recordings; what are the main differences between these techniques, and between their results?
- the conventions used in transcribing conversations (see Figures 6.10 and 6.11) and the two methods of setting out the transcription, the 'standard transcript' and the 'column transcript'. What are the advantages and problems of each method?

You can compare this explanation with the examples of transcribed conversation in Chapter 1, for example, in sections 1.2, 1.4 and the storytelling in 1.5.

Audiocassette 3 Band 5 Informal talk

(*Allow about 1 hour*)

Band 5 is a ready-made recording of a conversation for you to use. Try transcribing it using the methods described in *Describing Language*, and compare your attempts with the examples there and in Chapter 1. Full notes on the band and this activity are in the notes at the end of this guide; turn to them now and listen to the tape.

Overview of your work

(*Allow about 30 minutes*)

Finally, to help you in consolidating this week's work, look back to the study questions at the start of week 10's study notes. Check that you can answer them, and that you understand how this week's topics relate to the themes of the course. You are then ready to move on to week 11.

WEEK 11 LITERACY PRACTICES IN ENGLISH

Study questions

Keep these questions in mind as you work through the material. They will help you to focus on the issues raised this week and how they relate both to last week's work and to the themes of the course as a whole. At the end of this week's work, use them as a means of reviewing what you have learned.

Questions	**Related block themes**
What are the main differences between spoken and written English?	*Varieties of English*
How does the social and cultural context affect the form and style of written English and our response to texts?	*English in context/ achieving things in English*
How do our literacy practices allow us to create identities for ourselves as writers and literacy mediators?	*English and identity/ varieties of English/English in context*
How, and how far, are changes in social context and technology reflected in the genres and styles of our writing?	*Changing English/ achieving things in English*

Introductory study notes and study chart

The chart shows the components that you will need in working through this study week. We suggest that you study them in the order in which they occur in the chart.

Study chart for course week 11

Course book		*Set book*	
Chapter/teaching text	*Readings*	Describing Language	*Audiocassette 3*
2 Literacy practices in English	A Literacies among the Panjabis in Southall B Changing literacy in a South African informal settlement C Computer-mediated English: sociolinguistic aspects of computer-mediated communication		
			Band 6 Literacy in practice: letter writing in English and Kannada (linked to section 2.3 of the course book chapter)
		The following extracts: pp. 14–15; 19–20; 89–93; 196–7; sections 7.1, 7.2 and 7.4, pp. 219–24	
Review of week 11			

This week's topic continues the block's important theme of studying English in use. The focus now shifts from everyday speech to everyday uses of reading and writing. We consider the similarities and differences between these two modes. Chapter 2 of the course book opens up some significant issues, which are reinforced by a reading from *Describing Language.* We consider the influence of social and cultural context on the conventions we use in different genres of everyday writing and the changes that have occurred, and are occurring, in our literacy practices in response to changing circumstances and new technology. Through the chapter and its associated readings, we explore how we construct a range of writer identities for ourselves. This may be done as we write in different genres and as we move from one variety of language to another, both within English and in multilingual situations.

This range of uses emphasizes the varieties of English that the chapter considers, including: Indian literacy practices in the state of Karnataka and in a Panjabi family now living in the UK; Puerto Ricans in the USA; translation from English into Arabic; and the effects of changing literacy practices in a South African settlement. One of these examples, a letter from an Indian father to his daughter in Britain, is discussed further on Audiocassette 3 Band 5. The workload isn't as heavy as last week's, you'll be pleased to hear.

The notes below will take you through the components of study week 11 in the order in which they occur in the chart. It would be helpful to glance at the chart to see how these components fit together and then read the relevant notes for each component as you study it.

Course book Chapter 2 Literacy practices in English

(*Allow 6–7 hours*)

The chapter sets out the main topics for this week. Here are some suggestions to help you in your reading.

- As you read, keep comparing what the chapter says about writing and literacy practices with study week 10's views on everyday practices in spoken English; be aware of the similarities and differences between people's daily practices in speech and writing. There will also be links to next week's topic, 'English at work', so whenever you come across material in this week's study which is related to work, especially in section 2.5 on the literacy practices of the legal profession, keep it in mind. You will then be ready to relate it to the coming chapter and its ideas. In particular, we shall be having a further look at the work of the Plain English Campaign and at how their views compare with the English practices of some firms.
- Look out for the structural and grammatical features of the different genres of everyday written English in current use. Section 2.2 gives helpful comparisons between the characteristic forms of speech and writing in general. Section 2.5 brings in the theme of change through time, highlighting the changes in literacy practices over almost two centuries, with special reference to legal writing. It also looks ahead to current developments, which are likely to expand in the future, by exploring the impact of computer-mediated literacy practices on written English. You could contrast the linguistic forms described in Reading C as typical of computer-mediated communication with those set out at the beginning of the chapter. How far have you any experience of this type of communication? Does it relate to any literacy practices you currently use (e.g. surreptitious written notes to a colleague during a

meeting) or do you find it a new development? The influence of new technology on the future of English will be explored further towards the end of the course.

- A major theme of this chapter is the influence of social and cultural context on people's literacy practices. Reading A gives examples of a wide range of these influences in a multicultural setting. It is interesting and useful to compare such examples of writers conforming to the literacy conventions of their own culture, and of people acting as literacy mediators for others, with our own experiences as readers and writers. Think of the connection between this and the identities we create for ourselves as writers. (I'm conscious of this as I write these study notes; they're aimed to be something like the written equivalent of an informal phone discussion that I'd have with my own students about the course material. Although I don't know you personally, we share a common interest in understanding the ideas and material of the course. I've just used 'I' five times in three sentences – a high rate for academic-related writing.) Why not compare an extract from one of your recent TMAs with more informal writing of your own, like notes and letters, using the criteria from section 2.2?
- As the chapter points out, the context of a text is reflected in its form (for example, painted or electrical signs, computer printouts, scribbled notes on the back of an envelope), as well as in its content. You could compare this chapter with the discussion of the history of written English in Chapter 2 of the first course book. Block 6 will also offer some helpful parallels with the material in section 2.6 of this week's chapter, which deals with modern attitudes to illiteracy and difficulties with using written English.

Audiocassette 3 Band 6 Literacy in practice: letter writing in English and Kannada

(Allow about 45 minutes)

We are now going to take a closer look at a specimen of personal literacy practices in action. Band 6 is a discussion of the letter in English and Kannada, referred to in Section 2.3 of Chapter 2. The style of writing Kannada and English letters is more fully explored and Jaya explains her views on having two contrasting styles to use. We suggest that you work through the cassette band when you have read section 2.3, before going on to section 2.4. Or, if you prefer not to interrupt your reading, work through the band after reading Chapter 2.

You will find the study notes, and the text of the letter, in the audiovisual notes at the end of this guide. Please turn to those notes now, read them and listen to this band.

Describing Language Extracts

(Allow about 45 minutes)

This is a good point at which to make a more precise and detailed study of Halliday's model of language, which is frequently referred to in this block. To do this, you will need to check on the references to him and his work in *Describing Language.*

Please now read pages 14–15, 20 (and look back to 19, if you like, to understand the context), 89–93 and 196–7.

As you read, make brief notes on Halliday's ideas about language and how it works; try to put them in your own words, to make sure that you understand them.

After reading

You probably noted down the following points, among others.

From pages 14–15:

- His adoption of Malinowski's idea of the context of situation; the central importance of this idea in understanding the interlinking of the language that is used and the setting in which it is used.

From pages 19–20:

- The stress placed on studying language from existing spoken forms rather than from written examples.

From pages 89–93 (an important section):

- Language as a social and cultural phenomenon, responding to human needs; 'systemic-functional grammar' as a way of explaining how language is used to create meanings; the three key aspects of the context which it is necessary to analyse:
    - field: the topic of conversation and the activity which includes the conversation;
    - tenor: the nature of the relationship between the speakers;
    - mode: the channel of communication – for example, spoken, written, electronic, and the forms of grammar that have come to be associated with each of these.
- The complementary aspects of language – ideational, conveying ideas and information; interpersonal, building and maintaining relationships; textual, when both of these are combined in speech or writing.

From pages 196–7:

- The differences between speech and writing, which relate to Halliday's concept of mode.

Think back over Chapter 1 of the course book and see how these concepts help in explaining the nature of the conversations you have seen in this chapter. You may like to take one or more of the examples of conversation from the chapter, consider the field, tenor and mode of each and see how these affect the nature of the language used. You will also be able to do this as you read Chapter 3 on language in the workplace in week 12.

Describing Language Chapter 7, sections 7.1, 7.2 and 7.4

(Allow about 1 hour)

These further readings from *Describing Language* are also appropriate at this point; spend a little time reading and thinking about them.

You have already dipped into part of section 7.2 in the previous activity. It would now be useful to read sections 7.1 and 7.2 in full. They will expand the discussion of the differences between speech and writing, and the linguistic features which distinguish them. You could compare the list in Table 7.1 with the account of the differences given in the course book, Chapter 2, section 2.2. Also consider the view that a text, whether spoken or written, is not always confined to one mode, but may show characteristics of both speech and writing. Think back to Simeon Yates's views on computer-mediated communication in Reading C of Chapter 2 – perhaps look back at it to remind yourself of what he says.

The short extract on 'Political discourse analysis' (pp. 219–24) links to the previous discussion of language as a social activity. It extends the idea of the cultural context as a shaping force on the form and structure of language used in particular interactions. Look at the approaches of critical linguistics and critical language study to the examples that are given in the text; note the importance that these methods give to a conflict model of society and to discourse as a 'site of struggle' (p. 220) where participants are trying to establish their interpretation of the situation. Look again at the account of the minute-taking incident in Reading B of Chapter 2 in the light of this approach, and compare the way in which the minutes are expressed with the narrative techniques used in the newspaper stories in this extract, in terms of how the agency is stated or hidden. Look back at section 2.2 of Chapter 2 which discusses in full features such as nominalization and passive verb forms in written English and their effect of hiding agency.

Look out for these features of written style as you read your own newspaper.

Review of week 11

(Allow about 30 minutes)

To make sure that you have a clear understanding of the issues raised in this study week, and how they relate to the course themes, look back at the study questions given at the start of this week's study notes. Spend a few moments jotting down answers to them, and checking your ideas against the study material. You'll be picking up many of these points again in Block 4 and in the final blocks of the course. This is also a good point at which to watch TV 3 and work through the associated material if you have video-recorded it and haven't had time to watch it yet; you'll need it for week 12.

WEEK 12 ENGLISH AT WORK

Study questions

These are the main questions which this week's study addresses and the course themes to which they are related. Use them to focus your mind as you work through the material and study the examples of work-related language. You can then come back to them at the end of the study week and use them to summarize and review what you have learned.

Questions	Related block themes
How does the context of work create distinctive forms of English to suit the needs of the job?	*Achieving things in English/changing English: English in context*
Do work-related varieties share any common features?	*Varieties of English*
Does the use of work language create a special discourse community? If so, how?	*English and identity*

What are the main differences between work-related speech as used to fellow workers and to members of the public?	*Varieties of English/ achieving things in English*
How does work-related language compare with everyday conversation?	*Varieties of English/English in context*

Introductory study notes and study chart

For week 12 you will need the following components; we recommend that you work through them in the order shown in the chart.

Study chart for course week 12

Course book		*Set book*		
Chapter/teaching text	*Readings*	Describing Language	*Audiocassette 3*	*TV*
3 English at work	A Constructing the virtual building: language on a building site			TV 3 extract
	B Bear hugs and Bo Dereks on Wall Street			
	C Professionals and clients: form filling and the control of talk	Chapter 7, pp. 210–14		
			Band 7 English at work	
			Band 8 Work talk	
Review: Video Band 2 and review of study questions				
TMA 03				

This week's work continues and develops the theme of English in use. It provides a valuable contrast to the analysis of everyday conversation in week 10 and the study of our daily literacy practices in week 11, by moving the focus to the specific functions of English at work. Chapter 3 from the course book, which discusses the range of work contexts and the special features of English as a 'tool for the job', is supplemented by two bands on Audiocassette 3. One is a series of interviews which expand the range of views on the use of English at work as set out in the chapter. The second is an example of language in a work situation for you to study in detail. The workload is not too heavy this week, so you may like to look again at the section of TV 3 which relates to the use of an 'English Only' policy in the American meat-processing factory, for a comparison with section 3.2 of Chapter 3. You may also wish to start thinking about TMA 03, on the basis of what you have studied so far in this block.

This section of Block 3 is particularly concerned with using English to achieve goals, and the effect that this has on the structure of the language, in particular the specialized jargon that this use often generates. This is related to the theme of varieties of English, and to changes in these specialized forms to suit new work practices. Issues of context and identity in relation to the workplace and its language are important aspects of this week's work.

The notes below take you through the components in the order in which they are given above. It would be useful to look briefly at how they relate together and to read the notes for each component before you work through it.

Course book Chapter 3 English at work

(*Allow about 6–7 hours*)

This chapter is at the centre of this week's work. As you read it, keep the study questions in mind; the chapter offers valuable comparisons with the work on everyday conversation in week 10, and with week 13, when we shall consider another specific use of English, this time for purposes of persuasion.

Here are some suggestions to help in your reading:

- The chapter has a strong emphasis on the practical aspects of English. It stresses the way in which work-related English is as much part of the process of 'getting the job done' as are the actual techniques and materials that it refers to. Reading A, 'Constructing the virtual building', demonstrates this particularly clearly, and shows the importance of talk even in jobs where the main business is not concerned with manipulating words (compare road building with advertising, for instance).
- Look for the use of Halliday's ideas again – his concept of the *interpersonal* function of language as a means of building relationships in a work context, side by side with its *ideational* function of conveying information, explaining and negotiating. Halliday's view of the *intertextuality* of work-related discourse also features in this section. How far does this style of discourse help to create a 'discourse community' among fellow workers? Linguists have often grouped speakers together on the basis of some degree of common features in their use of language; you will find references to this in Chapter 3, as elsewhere in the course. You may also like to refer to *Describing Language* Chapter 1, pages 23–4, for a discussion of the (rather broader) notion of a *speech community*.
- If you're becoming interested in the structure of English, this chapter has plenty of material for you to work on. Look for the use of specialist jargons which answer the language needs of different workplaces, and how these change over time to fit changes in the work practices to which they relate. Reading B has some fascinating examples of the jargon of New York stockbrokers, for example. The chapter also considers how far individual jobs generate their own specific styles, such as the workers' speech in the Lancashire cotton mills earlier this century and the current development of 'police speak' as an Anglo-French venture.
- The use of specialist work-related language involves the significant issue of context, which the chapter engages with in some detail: the difference in the style of language used between colleagues at work, and between a professional and the general public. This raises issues of power and control; for example, the filtering and reformulation of the client's language by the professional for a range of purposes. Section 3.3 discusses this, and there is

further evidence in *Describing Language* Chapter 7 (see notes on this below). These issues are also relevant to gender relations at work and their influence on who controls the conversation. (You could relate this to Chapter 1's discussion of similar gender-related control in everyday conversation.)

- Another context-related issue is the use of English for trading purposes; this connects with the historical development of English pidgins and creoles which you studied in Blocks 1 and 2. You are also asked to consider the difference in use and response when business English is used between native speakers from similar cultural backgrounds and when one speaker uses it as a second language. A third situation, which the final block of the course may encourage you to think about again, is the growing use of English among workers and traders for whom it is not the first language. Why is it that workplace use of English seems to run smoothly in some of these cases but not in others? What other factors could be involved? Look carefully at the use of English at work in the garment industry of Macau and by Wipro Fluid Power in southern India, and the discussion on Spanish–English codeswitching in section 3.2. Audiocassette 3 Band 7 contains further discussion of workplace English, including an extract from an interview with Anil Kumar, from Wipro Fluid Power. TV 3's account of the problems encountered by an American food-processing company with its 'English Only' in the workplace policy is also relevant here.
- This chapter provides some good supporting evidence for the theme of varieties in English, in more than one sense. It shows us codeswitching; varieties of English such as pidgins; a range of world Englishes including varieties used by first and second language speakers, and different styles to suit the needs and the demands of workplace contexts and functions.
- Working through this chapter will probably make you aware of your own functional uses of English, related to work or to a specialist hobby or interest. You may like to take this study further, by observing your own use of jargon – how is this changing as its subject changes? Does your group use it to help in creating a discourse community connected with the activity? Is it ever used to exclude an 'outsider'? When you come to Block 7 of the course you will take up aspects of this subject again, as we look at the latest developments in prescripted forms of speech for workplace use in dealings with the public.

Review of TV 3 'English Only' in America

(*Allow about 25 minutes*)

This would be a good time to review TV 3 if you have been able to record the programme. The 'Spun steak' episode is particularly relevant to your work during this week, but the programme sets this in the wider context of debate and policy making at state level. As you watch the programme, note down any points that relate to the discussion in Chapter 3 of the course book, particularly section 3.2. In particular, note (a) the reasons given by the management of the food factory for insisting on the use of English in the workplace, and (b) the reasons the workers give for objecting to this policy. Bearing section 3.2 in mind, consider to what extent the functions of language in the workplace are given due consideration by management or workers.

Describing Language Chapter 7, pages 210–14

(Allow about 20 minutes)

This short section, which is part of the discussion of discourse analysis you began in week 10, offers another example of specialized work-related English, in this case the exchanges between teacher and pupils in the classroom. Teachers encourage dialogue between themselves and pupils, and between pupils, as part of the learning process; but it is a distinctive style of English, controlled and directed by the teacher and in many cases following a pre-set structural route, the so-called 'IRF structure'. The teacher knows the goals that the pupils are to achieve, and steers the conversation towards them, introducing the subjects and treating some of the subjects raised by pupils as irrelevant. In this way, the professional's control over the dialogue is asserted.

There is also some degree of reworking and reformulating of pupils' contributions to emphasize the desired responses and make use of them in the corporate movement of this conversation towards its specific goal. You may notice that the teacher's contributions are more precisely phrased and explicit than those used in some of Chapter 1's informal conversations, or than some of the worker-to-worker conversation in Reading A; why do you think this is? You can also compare this context with that of the doctor–patient interviews in this chapter. Think, for example, about the purposes behind the use of questions – the doctor aims to extract the information he or she needs – 'Does it hurt here?', 'How long have you been feeling sick?' – while the teacher is checking on what the pupil understands.

Audiocassette 3 Band 7 English at work

(Allow about 30 minutes)

Band 7 provides further comments on the language styles of the workplace. It contains three interviews, two with managers and one with a member of the Plain Language Commission, discussing new policies on the language to be used at work. You will find the study notes to accompany this band at the end of this guide. Please turn to them now, listen to this band and work through the activity suggested in the notes.

Audiocassette 3 Band 8 Work talk

(Allow about 45 minutes)

We suggest you now try your hand at making your own transcription and analysis of work-related talk. Please turn to the audiocassette notes at the end of this guide, then work through Band 8 on the audiocassette.

Review of week 12

(Allow about 1 hour 30 minutes)

This contains a two components: a video band and a review of this week's study questions.

Video Band 2 English at work

(Allow about 45 minutes)

To begin reviewing your work in week 12, we suggest you first watch Video Band 2 and work through the activity that goes with it. The detailed notes for this band are at the end of this study guide. Please turn to them now and read them, then watch Band 2.

Themes and study questions

(Allow about 45 minutes)

To complete your review, and bring together the main ideas you have encountered during this week, check that you can answer the study questions set out at the beginning of the study notes above.

TMA 03

It is a good idea to begin your preparations for TMA 03 during this study week. We suggest that you spend some time now looking back over your study so far in this block to select material that you want to use in answering your chosen question and to begin to organize this under relevant headings. You should keep in mind your TMA topic, and the material you have already gathered together, as you begin to work through week 13.

WEEK 13 RHETORIC IN ENGLISH

Study questions

These will help you in reviewing the work of this section and in bringing together the work of Block 3 by comparing this week's topic with those of the previous three weeks. Keep the questions in mind as you work through the material for study, and refer back to them at the end of the week.

Questions	**Related block themes**
What do the forms of public rhetoric discussed in this week – e.g. political, evangelical – aim to achieve?	*Achieving things in English/English in context*
What are the linguistic features that are used to help achieve these aims?	*Achieving things in English/English in context*
How far does the style of the public rhetoric analysed here differ from the examples of private persuasion? Are there any similarities?	*Varieties of English/English and identity*

Introductory study notes and study chart

Here is a list of the study materials you will need to work though week 13; we recommend that you study them in this order:

Study chart for course week 13

Course book		*Set book*		
Chapter/teaching text	*Readings*	Describing Language	*Audiocassette 3*	*Video*
4 Rhetoric in English	A Our Masters' Voices			
	B 'The light has gone out': Indian traditions in English rhetoric			
	C Televan-gelical language: a media speech genre			
		7.4 Written language (related to section 4.2 of the course book chapter)		
			Band 9 Rhetoric and persuasion	
Review: Video Band 3 and review of study questions				
Review of Block 3				

So far in Block 3 you have considered the everyday use of English in speech and writing, and its more specialized function as the language of work. In week 13 we move on to another specialized use of 'English in action': the language used to persuade and convince people, generally known as *rhetoric.* We encounter this type of language use in the speeches of politicians, the preaching of evangelists and the persuasive speech in our daily lives, from friends trying to convince us to believe a story that they are telling us, to salespeople offering us a wonderful bargain. You will be able to compare these distinctive uses of speech with the ones you met earlier in Block 3. The final block of the course will take up the theme of persuasion again and consider probable future developments in such forms of English.

Beginning with the history of rhetoric, and the changes that have occurred in it over time, we go on to look at the contexts in which rhetoric is customarily used, publicly at political meetings and in religious programmes on TV and privately to convince friends. We examine the variety of English that rhetorical speech represents, and also the range of varieties within it, depending on the cultural traditions of the speaker and audience. We consider the positioning of speaker and hearers in specific identities through the use of rhetorical language. A significant thread running through all the study material is the way in which speakers achieve things with English; here, the achievement is persuading others to share your point of view. The workload is comparatively light this week, as you will need time to work on TMA 03.

The notes below will take you through the study material in the order in which it appears in the chart above. Look at the notes for each component before you begin to study it.

Course book Chapter 4 Rhetoric in English

(Allow 6–7 hours)

Again this week, the chapter from the course book is the main feature of your work. As you read, keep the study questions in mind.

Here are some points to help in your reading.

- The chapter begins by defining rhetoric and looking at its long-established place in the English-speaking world. Robin Wooffitt's examples are taken from particular organizational and cultural contexts. As you study these, you may find it interesting to compare them with examples you have come across yourself in contexts with which you are familiar – for example, political or religious rhetorical language that you have observed personally or seen on TV. Consider how far his analysis, and the claims that he makes about different rhetorical styles and their audiences' responses to them, correspond to your experiences and observations.
- The chapter's analysis of rhetorical examples is based on the techniques of *conversation analysis.* You may like to look back to the section from *Describing Language* that you read in week 10 to remind yourself of the techniques and methods of this form of analysis (*Describing Language,* Chapter 7, section 7.3).
- As you read section 4.2 on the structure of classical Greco-Roman rhetoric, consider how this style has formed modern rhetoric in many parts of the world: you may think of examples such as speeches in legal cases or leading articles in newspapers. Pause at the end of section 4.2 to look at section 7.4 from *Describing Language* (particularly pp. 229–30). This extract enlarges on the explanation of the features of classical rhetoric and refers to an interesting modern example, relevant to OU essays! See the study note on this extract below.
- It is valuable to pick out the significant stylistic features of rhetoric in the contexts analysed here, as you work through section 4.3 and look at the extracts. Features such as three-part lists, contrasts and shifts in intonation, and a deliberately planned mirror image within a phrase are vital aspects of persuasive speech in many contexts. Notice how these act as signals to the audience to give a positive response, and under what circumstances this fails to happen. How does a speaker's failure to use the appropriate rhetorical structure contribute to his or her inability to gain the effect that the speech was working towards? Keep these features of rhetorical style in mind for your studies in Block 4. We shall be examining the use of language as art, in poetry and fiction, and you will also be able to see how far the creative artist uses similar devices. For example, the concluding line of a short poem can make its point by a balanced mirror image like that used by Alf Morris in Extract 9 – compare it with the lines from Emily Dickinson's 'My life closed twice before its close':

  > Parting is all we know of heaven,
  > And all we need of hell.
  >
  > (Johnson (ed.), 1960)

- Notice also the similarities and differences in the features of persuasive speech, as shown in the examples that Chapter 4 offers us. For example, you could compare the styles of the late twentieth-century British politicians with that of the Indian political orator. Look at how their methods of involving their listeners compare with the black Pentecostal preaching style, as discussed in the chapter. Think whether the difference in context between public preaching and speaking on TV (like the TV evangelists discussed in Reading C) affects the style and the relationship with the audience.

- In section 4.5 the focus moves to informal persuasion. Look at the use of rhetorical devices by the speakers to create for themselves an identity as ordinary persons, so that their strange experiences have a basis in normality. You could refer back to Janet Maybin's discussion of the way people incorporate reported conversation into their stories and adopt other 'voices' in everyday conversation (Chapter 1 section 1.6). Compare it with the use of 'relived' speech and circumstantial details in this chapter's narratives, to make the extraordinary events seem believable.
- The readings offer useful supportive case studies. Reading A looks at non-verbal support for spoken rhetoric, such as gestures and gaze, and how this can increase the impact of the spoken word. There is more on non-verbal support for speech in the reading from *Describing Language* in week 14. Reading A also highlights the importance of technological innovations such as teleprompter screens; you could place this alongside consideration of the impact of technology on written forms of English in Chapter 2. As you study the chapter and its associated readings, it is helpful to be aware that different aims and methods in analysing rhetorical speeches will emphasize different aspects of their style. For example, three-part lists may be present in a speech, but they may not be brought to our attention by an analyst who is looking for other features; think of this as you read Reading B. Reading C picks up the distinctive speech of TV evangelists, isolating the factors which indicate to the viewers that the programme is 'religious'. We are made aware of this form as a mixture between public and private forms, with TV evangelists' transitions between formal declarations and everyday speech. You could relate this to Simeon Yates's views on CMC as a 'mixed style' in Reading C of Chapter 2. You will also find some helpful comparisons with the discussion of advertising styles in Reading C of Chapter 4 when you watch TV 4 in Block 4, which deals with the use of different voices to create identities.
- You'll probably have noticed the interpersonal function of rhetoric, as well as its ideational function of conveying a political or religious message. Its emotive impact plays a significant part in binding together the believers, whether members of a political party or of a religious group of whatever faith. It has the same effects within a protest group with a strongly felt shared aim such as the protection of the environment.

Describing Language Chapter 7, section 7.4

(Allow about 20 minutes)

To complement your study of the course chapter, look briefly at *Describing Language*, section 7.4. This section discusses different ways of analysing written language, so it also complements your earlier work on transcribing and analysing speech. We suggest you skim the section to get a general sense of the topics it covers. Then read pages 229–30 ('Rhetorical and narrative structure') more carefully; this extract is particularly closely related to Chapter 4 in the course book. It develops the discussion of classical rhetorical form, and helps us to understand the origins of some of the conventions governing the way an idea, or a viewpoint, is presented in formal western settings. Look at the relationship of Ciceronian internal structure to the generic structure of a scientific paper. It may be familiar if you have a scientific background. (There will be more discussion of this formal ordering of academic language in Block 6.) Perhaps the previous paragraph may have more immediate relevance to you if you're preparing for TMA 03. You will recognize the structure of the familiar 'Discuss' type of OU essay question; is it any comfort to know that students have been struggling with such questions since classical times?

You will return to some of the other topics discussed in section 7.4 as part of your study of Block 4.

Audiocassette 3 Band 9 Rhetoric and persuasion

(Allow about 40 minutes)

This band contains two examples of rhetoric in action for you to listen to and analyse. Please now turn to the notes at the end of this study guide for details on the band and the revision activity connected with it, and listen to Band 9.

Review of week 13

(Allow about 1½ hours)

This review contains two elements: a video band and a revision of the main points made in the study material.

Video Band 3 Public speaking

(Allow about 45 minutes)

For the review of this week's work, we suggest that you begin by watching Band 3 of the video, which contains further examples of rhetoric. Your work on this band should help draw together some of the ideas addressed in the week. Look at the video notes at the end of this guide before watching Band 3.

Themes and study questions

(Allow about 45 minutes)

For the final review activity, check through the study questions for week 13 and jot down some answers to them. This will help you in summing up the material and ideas you have encountered this week, and in comparing it with the discussion of other forms of English in use in weeks 10–12.

REVIEW OF BLOCK 3

To consolidate the work of the whole four-week block, we suggest you go back to the beginning of the study guide. Read through the introduction to the block again, and look at the summary of the block's themes. Check that you are aware of the presence of these essential themes in the course material that you have studied in Block 3. You will then be ready to finish your work on TMA 03 and move on to Block 4.

AUDIOVISUAL NOTES

TV 3 'English Only' in America

Producer: *Anne Diack*

Academic consultant: *Janet Maybin*

(*Duration: 23 minutes; study time: about 1 hour*)

Before viewing

This programme is about a topic that is highly relevant to this block as well as later parts of the course: the use of English by non-native speakers. It is concerned with the growth since the 1980s in the USA of movements aiming to enforce the use of English, and only English, in American organizations such as schools and businesses, using legislation if necessary to impose this policy. The programme traces the reasons behind the growth of these movements, especially in California, a state with many bilingual minority groups, where the first moves have been made to give legal backing to an 'English Only' policy. In 1986, the Californian electorate voted by a majority of 73 per cent to pass a State Official English Language Amendment. By 1989, seventeen states had declared English their official language, and others are considering doing the same. However, some municipalities have reacted by declaring themselves multicultural or multilingual. The programme discusses the arguments offered in favour of the 'English Only' policy, and balances them against the views of Americans who see this policy as a threat to the identity and civil rights of bilingual speakers and contrary to the spirit of the US constitution. (One in eight Americans speaks a language other than English at home.)

Some background information

John Tanton, English Language Advocates: 'In this highly variegated nation, having a common tongue … is one of the forces to hold the thing together, and balance the centrifugal forces that tend to pull us apart.'

- These are the main pressure groups on both sides of the issue, and their chief points of policy:

  'English Only' was the policy adopted in the 1980s by several organizations whose aims were to persuade the US government to add an 'English Language Amendment' to the National Constitution, which would make English the country's official language. The phrase 'English Only' was replaced in the late 1980s by the less exclusive-sounding term 'Official English'. Policy statements by pro-English groups make it clear that they do not oppose the use of other languages privately at home, or the teaching of foreign languages in school.
- One of the first campaigning groups was 'US English', founded in 1983 by Senator Hayakawa and John Tanton. It opposed the use of any language but English as the teaching medium in schools and for communication in other public-sector services like health and social services. This group is still actively campaigning and its current director, Mauro Mujica, appears in TV 3.
- Recently, some of the original 'US English' members have left the group to form a new organization, 'English Language Advocates' which is also campaigning for an English Language Amendment; it aims to cut back publicly financed bilingual services and to prevent Puerto Rico from becoming a state

of the USA unless it accepts English as its official language (over 60 per cent of Puerto Ricans do not speak English). John Tanton and Gerda Bikales, whose views you hear in the programme, are both founding members of 'English Language Advocates'.

- Another campaigning group, closely connected with the US Republican party, is 'English First', represented in the programme by Jon Stoos, speaking in San Francisco.
- The significant phrase used by the opposing groups in the area of education is 'English Plus'. This stands for their belief that while English is obviously extremely important, bilingual children should also have the opportunity to develop, and learn through, their other languages. The 'English Plus' policy, which is mentioned by the primary school headmaster in TV 3, promotes the learning of English by speakers of other languages in addition to their first language, and of other languages by native English speakers. (There is more discussion of language learning in Blocks 5 and 6.)
- Another reaction against the 'Official English' movement has come from civil liberty and advocacy groups. A leading example of these is MALDEF, the Mexican American Legal Defence and Educational Fund, whose aim is 'to protect and promote the civil rights of the over 24 million Latinos' living in the USA. MALDEF has campaigned actively against 'Official English' policies, and in TV 3 Martha Jimenez, a Mexican American attorney, explains why the organization sees the issues involved as so important. Another agency which has been involved in court battles to protect the bilingual rights of individuals in the workplace is the American Council for Civil Liberties, represented in TV 3 by Edward Chen who worked on the 'Spun steak' case described in the programme.

Gerda Bikales: '[Bilingual education] means the untying of the cultural bridges which in this country we've had to build.'

Martha Jimenez, MALDEF, 'It's easier to say to someone we don't like you because you don't learn English rather than to say we don't like you because you're Mexican, or you're Haitian ... because of the colour of your skin.'

As you watch the programme, ask yourself:

- What does it say about the rights of individuals and minority groups to use their first language?
- How does it relate language to personal and cultural identity?
- What are the main arguments put forward by each side in defence of their case?
- How does this state of affairs compare with language policies in any English-using country with which you are familiar?

Listen carefully to the narrator's closing words, which underline some of the controversial issues of language and nationality.

After viewing

Some points you might have picked out to consider:

- while the supremacy of English in the USA has not been questioned, it has never been formally or legally established as the official national language;
- the speaking of English is connected with the dominant, numerically bigger and wealthier groups in American society: one of the arguments put forward was that immigrants come to the USA to make money and they can do so more successfully by using English.

Arguments advanced by the various supporters of an 'Official English' policy include:

- the cost of providing bilingual education;
- the divisive effect of bilingual education, which is seen as fragmenting society and opposing the creation of common ideals; immigrants have come

Edward Chen, American Civil Liberties Union, '[English Only rules] interfere with basic human rights of language minorities to get access to the ballot box, to education, and to fundamental governmental services.'

from many countries and cultures, so English is seen as the common bond which unites them, and if they do not adopt English, this can lead to their segregation within society;

- by extension, the implication that support for the use of English is an indicator of patriotism; the president of the food company describes his fight to insist on English as 'carrying the flag';
- the fear of the loss of English in the face of the 'huge immigration' of non-English speakers, and so the loss of the culture associated with it; supporters of 'English First' claim that immigrants are refusing to learn English and so to take on American identity;
- the value of an 'English Only' policy at work in promoting harmony and safety within the organization and protecting the quality of the product.

Arguments against this point of view include:

- insisting on an English Only educational system disadvantages children whose first language is not English;
- it deprives them of the educational background they have already gained in their own language and disparages the culture to which they and their parents belong;
- it deprives people of their civil rights, such as taking part in elections;
- it can be used as a cover for racial discrimination and anti-immigration policies;
- the use of the English language is not a fundamental part of the American constitution and of the rights and duties connected with it as part of citizenship; the constitution is not based on language or religion but on the concept of individual liberties and on a common belief in a set of political principles.

As you can see, this debate raises some vital issues for the question of language and identity, both personal and cultural, and for the relationship between linguistic diversity and membership of nations and of speech communities. This is a serious issue in many countries today, not just in America; how far can or should we assume that membership of a nation or culture requires the use of one language rather than another? How far is language identical with culture? What about the paradox raised on the programme by one member of an 'Official English' group who said that 'all languages and cultures are precious and should be preserved' while at the same time insisting on the primacy of one language and its culture over all other minority languages? How far can two or more languages co-exist equally? These, and other related questions will be addressed in this block and also in later parts of the course; keep them in mind as you move into the coming weeks.

You will be referred to TV 3 in several of the weeks of Block 3, and asked to compare the views expressed in it with issues that arise from the course book chapters.

Suggestions for further reading

Two edited collections, including various points of view, are:

ADAMS, K.L. and BRINK, D.T. (eds) (1990) *Perspectives on Official English: the campaign for English as the official language of the USA*, New York, Mouton de Gruyter.

CRAWFORD, J. (ed.) (1993) *Language Loyalties: a source book on the Official English controversy*, Chicago, University of Chicago Press.

Other relevant books and papers include:

BARON, D. (1990) *The English-only Question: an official language for Americans?* New Haven, Connecticut, Yale University Press.
CRAWFORD, J. (1992) *Hold your Tongue: bilingualism and the politics of 'English Only'*, Wokingham, Addison Wesley.
MARSHALL, D. (1986) 'The question of an official language: language rights and the English Language Amendment' in *International Journal of Language*, vol. 60, pp. 7–75. (Explains the historical and contemporary context.)
NUNBERG, G. (1989) 'Linguists and the Official Language Movement', *Language*, vol. 65, no 3.

AUDIOCASSETTE 3

Producers: *Anne Diack* and *Paul Manners*

Academic consultants: *Janet Maybin* and *Neil Mercer*

Band 1 Introduction

Contributors: *Janet Maybin* and *Neil Mercer*, both from the Open University

(*Duration: approximately 2 minutes; study time: about 5 minutes*)

Janet Maybin and Neil Mercer explain the purpose of the cassette and the nature of the material you will hear on it. There are no additional notes for this band.

Bands 2–5 accompany Chapter 1 of the course book and form part of week 10.

Band 2 Aboriginal English

Contributors: *Diana Eades*, from the University of New England, Armidale, New South Wales, and *Janet Maybin*, from the Open University
(*Duration: 12 minutes; study time about 25 minutes*)

Diana Eades

Before listening

On this band you will hear Diana Eades, the Australian linguist who is also the author of Reading A in Chapter 1 of the course book, talking to Janet Maybin. Diana's main area of research is the variety of English used among Aboriginal people in Australia. She is particularly interested in differences in conversational styles and the difficulties they can cause for Aboriginals involved in court cases in the Australian legal system; this has led her to campaign on behalf of a number of Aboriginal defendants.

This band is intended to expand and develop the ideas that Diana Eades sets out in Reading A. She discusses how Aboriginal English differs from Standard Australian English in two significant areas. Listen carefully to her discussion of these and jot down what she says about:

- the differences in terms of linguistic features – pronunciation, grammatical structures and vocabulary;
- the differences in conversational style and why this can cause problems in the courts for Aboriginal speakers.

After listening

Some features you might have noticed are:

- the lack of differentiation of /b/ and /f/;

- the expression of possession by placing two nouns side by side; 'Jim foot' was the example she gave;
- the use of local Aboriginal words for certain areas of vocabulary such as parts of the body or taboo subjects.

In the discussion of conversational style you will have heard her take up the point, made in Reading A, about the Aboriginal use of indirectness in speech as a means of maintaining some privacy in a very public lifestyle. Direct questions are avoided; Aboriginal speakers prefer a leisurely-paced, ongoing dialogue in which the enquirer contributes his or her own information. Diana also pointed out the use and value of periods of silence as part of a conversation, used for reflection and as part of the establishment of social relationships. Her third area of difference was the use of agreement – what she called 'the "yes" of gratuitous concurrence' – where speakers agree to what is being said, not because it is true but to avoid open disagreement and keep the conversation moving smoothly. These obviously cause misunderstandings in the context of the conventions of behaviour in court; indirectness is interpreted as evasion. The silence can also be seen in this way, or as a sign of ignorance, and the 'yes' is taken as a sign of assent to the accuracy of what has been said.

Janet Holmes

Band 3 Hedges and tag questions

Contributors: *Janet Holmes,* from Victoria University, Wellington, New Zealand, introduced by *Janet Maybin*

(*Duration: 3 minutes; study time: about 30 minutes*)

Before listening

This is another interview with a focus on a South Pacific variety of English; it has links with Band 2 and with the examples of Aboriginal English on Band 4.

Janet Holmes, a New Zealand sociolinguist and Reader in Linguistics at Victoria University, is the author of Reading B in Chapter 1. The research that she describes here was begun in response to Robin Lakoff's work on 'women's language'. She set out to investigate the relationship between gender and features of conversational style. Her main interest is 'hedges'; look out for the specifically New Zealand features she describes:

- the use of *eh?* (She calls this an 'invariant tag', one that doesn't change its form whatever the question is, unlike forms such as *isn't she?, aren't we?*);
- the use of the 'high rising terminal' inflection at the end of a phrase.

You have met both features before: remember from Block 2 that invariant tags such as *isn't it?* are found in certain other varieties of English. Chapter 6 in the first course book (*English: history, diversity and change*) discusses this feature, and S.K. Verma provides an illustration from India on Audiocassette 2 Band 2. The high rising terminal is the same feature as the 'high rising tone' found in Australian English and discussed in week 7, in Chapter 7 of the first course book – different researchers have confusingly used different terms to refer to the same feature.

Listen for Janet Holmes's description of the relationship between the use of these features and gender and ethnic origins in New Zealand. Notice the connections between her findings and those of Allan Bell in his discussion of Maori and Pakeha pronunciations on Audiocassette 2 Band 5.

Note:

- you will remember from Allan Bell's talk that a 'Pakeha' is a New Zealand person of Anglo-European origins;
- 'Maori' is pronounced by Janet in the New Zealand way; listen particularly carefully to the /r/ sound.

After listening

Did you pick up Janet Holmes's interesting conclusions? They were:

- that both the *eh?* and the high rising terminal inflection are more commonly used by women among Pakeha New Zealanders;
- that they are used by both men and women in the Maori community; they therefore serve as Maori identity markers, especially among men;
- that they can serve as interactive devices, encouraging response and cooperation, both qualities prized in the Maori community.

Band 4 Aboriginal data

Contributors: *Lorina Barker* and *Karen Johnson* from Bourke in western New South Wales, Australia

(*Duration: 5 minutes; study time: about 1 hour*)

Lorina Barker

Before listening

This band gives examples of Australian Aboriginal use of English for you to analyse. The speakers are two young Australian Aboriginal women, Lorina and Karen. They are discussing their memories of schooldays and sharing their dislike of cane toads. The conversation was recorded at the University of Armidale, where Lorina is now a student.

As this conversation was recorded in a studio it was not easy for them to relax completely into the informal speech styles that they would use at home, but they still use a number of features of Aboriginal English as discussed on Band 2 and some of the features that Janet Holmes identified on Band 3. Listen carefully to the tape. We suggest you play it once to familiarize yourself with the accent and subject matter; then play the band again, stopping and starting as necessary, and then try to jot down:

- any specific features of Aboriginal English as identified by Diana Eades on Band 2;
- any use of the collaborative speech identified by Janet Holmes on Band 3, such as the tag 'eh?' or the high rising terminal inflection at the end of a phrase;
- any devices of conversational support, like agreement;
- how far the structure of their stories, especially the one about the cane toad, relates to Janet Maybin's discussion of narrative in Chapter 1.

To give you practice in analysing conversation by listening, it's best to try at first with only the tape. When you have tried this, look at the transcript of the conversation below. Listen to the tape again with this in front of you and see if you can add to your list of features.

Transcription of conversation between two young Aboriginal women, Lorina and Karen

Transcription conventions:

- (…) indicates incomprehensible speech
- deep brackets [indicate overlapping speech
- / is used where one utterance is latched on to the next, without a pause

Some punctuation has been added, to help comprehension

Lorina: 'Igh school was all right, I reckon, in Bourke

Karen: Yeah it used to be good when we all, when all our friends, but they all dropped out

Lorina: Like, well I was, I was about the last one left out of all my friends at at 'igh school, so

Karen: You went right through, we all pull out

Lorina: It was sort of lonely, actually, like I was, I was left there and I was sort of like wanting to get pull out then, and I stayed, sort of like there was no one else you can talk to, so (...)

Karen: I reckon it was good there, at first, in year seven when we first went, we thought we was real big there too (laughter). (…) Maybe not, in year seven, eh.

Lorina: All these big, all these other g- fellas eh, all the other kids. (em) Those days out on the ramp, sitting out there in recess you know, sitting out in the sun out in winter time.

Karen: Sit down there, never used to move there, didn't like moving out of the sun

…

Karen: I used to like science.

Lorina: Yea, I used to like science in year eight. It was good.

Karen: And art. Remember the big ship what I done?

Lorina: In art

Karen: They 'ad it right near the office there.

Lorina: Art, yea. You know them faces you know what we, what we made, those ugly old maché one, in year eight?

Karen: Oh, remem remember out (…) Weel, eh? That was a good, it was good when we was out there.

Lorina: In Weel, [yea

Karen: [yea, and the horses used to wait for us there, eh?

Lorina: Oh yea they used to chase us [to school every day

Karen: [run up the tree we used to.

Lorina: Those horses were terrible. Remember that day when you got um when [he chased ya

Karen: [chase me on the motorbike, eh?

Lorina: And that red 'ide or what that tanned 'orse and then we went back to get that cabbage patch doll, eh?

Karen: Yea [(…)

Lorina: [And then they chased us again. God, that was terrible (...)

Karen: Yea, an' that big pig, remember?

Lorina: Ahh- was he, what, what was he name? Um

	[(...)
Karen:	[I forgot he name
Lorina:	Oink, that was he name (laughter)
...	
Lorina:	I remember when we went up there one Christmas to Coochie Island and there's cane toads (...) there's cane toads, those ugly little things, you got to watch them [cause they jumping all over the place
Karen:	[Oh, what they look like?
Lorina:	They're big, [real big, ugly big face
Karen:	[Oh, ugly big frogs
Lorina:	And they just like they all over the place, they just sitting out there, you know you can at the windows, you can see 'em there, (oh) they jumping around everywhere, looking at you through the windows/
Karen:	/Oh, I seen this real big frog out Casino there
Lorina:	That's probably one of the cane toad/
Karen:	/No, he was a big green one, he was that long, and big, err, and just give me cold shivers
Lorina:	Ah you should see those cane toads there. I'm real frightened of 'em too cause they reckon they poisonous when if you – if they bite you or something/
Karen:	/Yea? They bite you?/
Lorina:	/Yea, I nearly treaded on one [once
Karen:	[Lock jaw or what?/
Lorina:	/I don't know, I don't know, I wouldn't want to touch them anyways/
Karen:	/eer they're 'orrible. We was looking at them once/
Lorina:	/We was walking on the beach, like you go it's like, when you go up there's like steps going up, and we was walking along the beach this night, and we walked up, me and Jason, and then, coming up there's sort of like a lot of grass, and all that near the, near the steps and this thing jumped out in front of me, I started screaming, 'A cane toad, a cane toad!' and I, I said 'Get him off! Come and let's hurry up!' and there's like, you got to watch where you're going to cause there's a lot smashed on the road where the cars run over 'em!

After listening

I'm sure you spotted some of the following Aboriginal features:

- A juxtaposed possessive in the discussion of the big pig; both women use the phrase *he name* where the standard form would be *his name.*
- *They poisonous* – a typical Aboriginal English verb omission; the auxiliary verb is omitted in *they just jumping all over.*

- You may want to argue that the use of *Maybe not* after an opinion on Year 7 is typical of the hedging of opinion rather than giving a direct statement.
- Some features are common to Aboriginal English and nonstandard Australian English, such as *we was* and *them faces what we made* (you may recognize similarities with other nonstandard varieties of English) and the omission of h in *'igh school.*
- *eh?* was used several times, e.g. in *all these other fellas, eh?* and in the comments about the horses, *and then we went back to get that cabbage patch doll, eh?*
- The high rising tone occurred frequently, especially in the story about the cane toads; is it particularly needed here to ensure interaction during a very long turn by one speaker? You probably included *if they bite you or something, there's like steps going up; where the cars run over them.* If you didn't find it easy to spot examples of this, listen again to this section of the band.

You no doubt noticed other supportive features, such as implicit references to shared experiences, *that big ship what I done*, incomplete phrases, cutting in, overlapping and completing each other's statements.

Band 5 Informal talk

Contributors: *Pip* and *Phyllis,* a married couple from south-east England

(*Duration: 4 minutes; study time: about 1 hour*)

Before listening

On this band is a recording of a conversation for you to use. Try transcribing this using the methods described in section 6.4 of *Describing Language.* To help you, look at the examples in section 6.4 and in the course book, Chapter 1, sections 1.2 and 1.4.

This conversation is between Pip and Phyllis, who have been married for 46 years. They have therefore had long practice in conversing with each other; they have a great deal of shared background knowledge, and are used to collaborating with each other. They have just had a weekend holiday break in Rome, and they are working together to fill in an evaluation form for the tour company with which they travelled.

This is the form:

To help us maintain our standards we would be grateful if you could complete and return this questionnaire.

RESORT VISITED

HOTEL/APARTMENT NAME

DEPARTURE DATE ______
NUMBER OF NIGHTS ______
DEPARTURE AIRPORT ______

PLEASE RATE EACH OF YOUR HOLIDAY COMPONENTS *(Tick Box)*

	EXCELLENT	V.GOOD	GOOD	FAIR	POOR
FLIGHTS					
FERRY or RAIL					
HOTEL Service					
Room facilities					
Location					

ADDITIONAL COMMENTS ______

NAME ______ ADDRESS ______

Thank you for your help

Listen to this band a couple of times, in order to familiarize yourself with the conversation. Then choose a short section and try to transcribe it using the format and conventions explained in *Describing Language*. If you get really interested, you could work through the whole conversation – it's quite short.

Don't worry if you don't find it easy; having a try helps you to understand the process of transcription and the problems of recording and analysing everyday conversation.

Then, from your transcript and also from the rest of the taped conversation, look for these characteristic features of informal conversation:

- any unfinished phrases or clauses;
- one speaker cutting in on the other just before a transition relevance point;
- duetting (both speaking together or collaborating to complete a phrase);
- back-channel support (short agreements like 'yes', 'mm');
- imprecise or inexplicit references which rely on their shared experience for understanding.

As you do so, think back to the claims in Chapter 1 of the course book that men tend to control mixed-gender conversations, choose the topics and give less conversational support. How far is this apparent in this extract?

After listening

There were several unfinished phrases, such as Pip's: *You had to well,* and *A leaflet like the one that er yes.* They cut in on each other's comments regularly; a good example was: *The 27th of //Right//April.*

Both of them gave support to the other, with comments like Phyllis's *That's right, Yes,* and *No, it wasn't* (in agreement with Pip's disapproval) and Pip's briefer but often used *Yes* and *mm.* There were also tags like, *Wasn't it?* (see Band 3). You probably also noticed the imprecise, and sometimes incomplete, references to shared memories, such as *In Paris that time,* and *I saw the coaches.* Most of these are features of collaborative conversation. You may well have found others in addition to these examples.

There are three main ways in which this conversation could be controlled: through speech – for example, by introducing topics, asking questions, making more complete utterances; through non-verbal means like body language and eye contact; by controlling the circumstances – for example, being the one who actually fills in the form.

We can discount the non-verbal means, as we can't work them out from an audio recording (although we could from a videotape). At first hearing, we could claim that Pip (the man) has more control. He is the one who is writing on the form, therefore he asks more direct questions. He also sets the structure at the beginning and regularly brings the conversation back to the task of answering the form's questions. So does this mean that he is in control? Not necessarily: we see that Phyllis takes a full part in the discussion. She often takes the lead in topics, suggests further information, interrupts and insists on her valuation being the one to be written down (the room was *good,* not *very good,* for example.) Sometimes they work in a collaborative way, giving support, changing their views, negotiating answers. After all, they have had plenty of practice in conversation with each other. Perhaps this explains the lack of disturbance caused by the frequent interruptions; they often talk at the same time, but it doesn't seem to bother them. Does each know, by now, what the other is going to say?

Don't forget that Pip and Phyllis, like Lorina and Karen, the Aboriginal women on Band 4, are aware that they are being recorded. It is not always easy to be relaxed and spontaneous in these circumstances, and speakers don't always use the speech forms that they might employ in normal circumstances. Perhaps you've experienced this yourself if you've taken part in a tape recording.

Band 6 Literacy in practice: letter writing in English and Kannada

Contributors: *G.D. Jayalakshmi*, a BBC producer and contributor to several parts of the course, talking to *Janet Maybin*

(*Duration: 6 minutes; study time: about 45 minutes*)

Before listening

This band is closely related to the discussion of the letter in English and Kannada in section 2.3 of the course book chapter. Listen to Band 6, with the text of the letter to Jaya in front of you, to help you understand the references in the taped discussion.

Janet Maybin from the course team discusses the letter with G.D. Jayalakshmi (whom you heard on Audiocassette 2 talking about codeswitching). Look back at Chapter 2, Activity 2.3 for an explanation of the background to Jaya's family's literacy practices and her father's interest in helping her and her young family to extend their literacy in Kannada. The letter, in both languages, reflects the cultural background of Jaya and her family; her husband is Scottish and they are bringing up their triplets in England to be bilingual. She came to the OU to do a PhD and now works as a BBC producer for the OU. She still keeps her cultural roots in India and in the shared use of Kannada with her father. The discussion makes it clear that he is keen for Jaya's children to learn the language and share this aspect of their culture; she mentions that he includes in his letter little stories and some words for them to learn.

As you listen to the cassette and look at the letter, note down what features of the letter strike you as particularly formal. How does the English section of the letter compare with the blessings and greetings in Kannada (translated for you in Activity 2.3)? What comparisons does Jaya make between letters in Kannada and letters written by Indians in English? What does she say about the use of the two written conventions and her perception of her personal identity?

Jaya (in the foreground) with members of her family: her brother, Jaggu, her mother, Sukanya and her father, Swamy

ॐ

श्रीराम

M. S. S. Swamy
(Retd. Dy. Chief Engineer
SAIL-Bokoro Steel Plant)
CONSULTANT
M/s. ASIAN TECHS LTD.
P. B. No. 3512, M. G. Road,
ERNAKULAM.
COCHIN-PIN. 682035.

Date 22nd May '94

[illegible] (Donald) [illegible] (Hari), [illegible] (Neel) [illegible] (Shona) [illegible] (best wishes)

Well, both chi. Sow. Sukanya and I, are very pleased to learn that the children liked the toys I posted. This time I have sent a few books which they may like. We are pleased to learn that Dr. Lakani was very much impressed by their progress in speech (the children). We are also happy to learn that they are standing erect and trying to move around in the erect posture. We are eagerly awaiting to see their latest photos. Tour chi. Ry. Jaggu has safely landed in GAINSVILLE, we heard that he landed safely at New-York and had to stay there for the night as he did not have time to catch his flight to Orlando. Perhaps, he must have reached his destination safely by Sat. evening (American time). He may join his duties as per schedule on 23/5/94 by the grace of God.

May God bless you all. Pl. reply

I have noted below some of the most important festivals for your information. Your BBC calender also gives the details.

Date	Festival
25/5/94	Buddha Purnima. (Wednesday)
21/8/94.	Raksha - Bandhan (Sunday)
28/8/94	Sri Krishna Janmastami (Sunday)
8/9/94.	Sri. Swarna-Gowri Puja (Thursday)
9/9/94	Sri GANESHA Puja (Friday)
6/10/94 to 14/10/94	NAVA RATRI DURGA-PUJA.

(10th Oct - Saraswati Puja, 12th Oct - Durga Puja, 13th Oct - Maha Navami and 14th Oct Vijaya Dasami.

2nd Nov 94 – Deepavali (South Indian custom)
3rd .. 94 – Diwali (North India)

With our love + blessings yours ever loving parents/grand parents
M.S.S. Swamy

Letter from Jaya's father

After listening

You will have noticed Jaya's comments on the relative formality of all Kannada letters, which is reflected in her father's use of the traditional formulae and the comparatively formal phrasing, by western English standards, of the section in English. She claims that the traditional format of the Kannada letter has influenced her style of writing to fellow Indians in English; she always uses some formal greeting phrases to begin such a letter. You probably also picked up her mother's role as a literacy mediator for Jaya as a child and the way in which Jaya is now repeating that role by reading the letters to her own children. The issue of identity in relation to cultural context emerges clearly in Jaya's determination to keep her footing in both Indian and western cultures. As she says, 'The more identities you have, the better it is.'

This letter will make a valuable comparison with your own literacy practices. Spend a few moments comparing it with any letters you may have received from your own family and friends.

If you can find letters, whether recent or from some time ago, from a range of generations, for example, from grandparents, parents, your own or friends' children, so much the better. You may like to include a letter that you are in the process of writing to friends or family. Look at the conventions used: the forms of opening and closing; the signature; any formulae of greeting; the choice of vocabulary and syntax; whether full sentences or incomplete phrases are used; abbreviations; punctuation (how many exclamation marks, for example?); the variety of English used – is it all in Standard English? Does it include any codeswitching between varieties of English, or between English and another language?

Ask yourself why these particular features are used and how far they reflect the social and cultural context and the conventional practices of the writers. Also consider how far the differences you have noticed are related to the age group to which the writer belongs. You may notice elements of both. (If you try to write a personal letter immediately after doing this activity, you'll find yourself analysing everything you write for evidence of your literacy practices!)

Band 7 English at work

David O'Brien

Contributors: *Neil Mercer* from the course team and author of Chapter 3 introduces the following speakers:

David O'Brien is a former managing director of Rank Xerox in the UK; he then became chief executive of the National Provincial Building Society.

Anil Kumar holds a similar position in Bangalore in the southern Indian state of Karnataka; he is a senior manager at Wipro Fluid Power, an engineering company which manufactures hydraulic cylinders.

Martin Cutts was one of the co-founders of the Plain English Campaign and has since established an organization with similar aims, the Plain Language Commission. He also runs Words at Work, an editing and training consultancy. He is particularly interested in simplifying legal English.

(Duration: 12 minutes; study time: about 30 minutes)

Before listening

This band reinforces the ideas about language at work which are explained in the course book chapter. It looks further at the two main aspects of workplace language: English within the organization, for the purposes of getting the job done, and the parallel function of communicating with the public as clients and customers. It will help you in reviewing the main themes of this study week. We suggest that you listen to the three interviews separately first, to establish the speakers' ideas; you may then like to listen to the band again, comparing their views.

As you listen to the tape, keep these questions in mind and jot down your responses to them:

- What changes did David O'Brien introduce into the language used by the building society, and why?
- Why did Wipro Fluid Power decide on English as the workplace language? What exceptions are allowed, and why?
- What are Martin Cutts's objections to traditional legal language, and what alterations does he suggest?

If you have become interested in the use of jargon at work, you may enjoy collecting the examples of 'writing to impress' and reduplicated legal language which Martin Cutts gives.

Anil Kumar

Martin Cutts

After listening

You probably noticed the changes made in the workplace vocabulary. Perhaps the most significant was the move from *job* with its connotations of a firm place within the organization, to *role* with its suggestion of flexibility and change – we speak of *adopting a role* or *playing a role* with the implication that we can move quickly and easily from one role to another. The two other major changes from traditional business language are the change from *skills* which went with *job* to *competences* for the *role*, and the move from the usual *meeting* to *event* with its suggestion of something significant happening. David O'Brien claims that these changes will help in the modernization of a traditional organization, reflect the changes in it and ensure understanding of exactly what the new developments mean. In the light of his final comment at the end of this band, how far do you think his new language policy reflects his structural changes and fulfils a workplace need? How far might it simply generate new jargon in its turn?

You could remind yourself at this point of the reading from Chapter 4 of *Describing Language*, which you read in week 4 and reviewed in week 9. It discussed the importance of context in determining the meaning of a word, and this is relevant to David O'Brien's views as expressed on this band. How far do all users of English agree on the exact meaning of *job* and *role*, of *meeting* and *event* and of the precise differences between them? Can we be certain that the connotations of each of these words will be the same in all circumstances and for all listeners, or will they be affected and determined by people's varied previous experiences of these words in different contexts? If so, what are the implications for a company language policy like David O'Brien's?

English was chosen as the workplace language for internal transactions in the offices of Wipro Fluid Power, according to Anil Kumar, to ensure efficiency because of the confusion caused by different local languages spoken by the workforce. It is also a valuable means of communication with outside organizations such as customers and suppliers and the state government. As Chapter 3 explains, English is used for official writing such as employees' contracts and job specifications, instructions for operating machinery and records of work. These details below about the company's policy will help to fill out the picture.

English is spoken in formal contexts such as meetings and training courses, and informally among the staff. Employees have all learned English at school; they then take a four-month training course in English when they join the company, and they are encouraged to increase their self-confidence in using English by reading widely and watching English language TV. The local state language, Kannada, is used for informal speech between shopfloor workers. On occasions, it is used between them and managers: for example, any disciplinary procedures are written down in English, but they will be explained to the employee in Kannada, to ensure that they are fully understood. For the same reason, company standing orders concerning matters like employment and conduct are displayed on the notice boards in both English and Kannada. Kannada is used for social events such as the company's Karnataka Rajyotsava festival, when employees' families come to enjoy sports and a celebration of local culture and language. There have been some objections to this policy from the unions, and also from the state government, which recently stated that all written communications with it should be in Kannada; this has been resisted by a number of local companies, including Wipro. However, the company's policy on the use of English at work has been generally accepted.

The shop floor at Wipro Fluid Power

Martin Cutts, like David O'Brien, is interested in modernizing obsolete language, although he does so for different reasons and in other ways. He picked out the traditional double, and even triple, phrases used in legal documents, like *give, devise and bequeath* whose former function of specifying different kinds of property has now gone, and synonyms like *null and void*. His group suggests pitching the language at an appropriate level for its readers, some of whom may have trouble with English. He also recommends breaking up long sentences. (I'm watching mine carefully, as a result!) He prefers using active rather than passive verb forms and avoiding the involved professional jargon which he calls 'legalese' by choosing common words rather than unusual ones.

Martin Cutts is keen to point out some of the effects of different styles of writing:

> Writing is one of the most highly visible and permanent indicators of competence. The client's memory of your likeable and supportive demeanour may fade, but he will always be able to open his case file and ponder the exact words you have written. Your reputation rides out with every letter you send.
>
> Skilful and speedy drafting should be among all lawyers' greatest assets. Many spend 30–50% of their working time producing the written word; they are professional writers. But is enough quality work being harvested from this huge investment? Do established lawyers and new recruits produce intelligible, crisp, cogent English? Perhaps it would be surprising if they did, for the skills of better and faster writing are neither widely taught in law schools nor easy to acquire on the job. When the legal correspondent of *The Times* attended London magistrates' courts in 1979 to assess the quality of service, he was appalled that 'so many young barristers seemed incapable of forming a grammatically correct English sentence' (*New Law Journal*, 15 Nov 79, p. 1117). My experience, gained during writing courses for solicitors, is that the picture is not quite as black as that. But letters like this one, sent to a client who had complained of errors and overcharging, still abound:
>
> > We beg to refer to the above matter and are in receipt of your correspondence of the 28th ultimo, the contents of which have been noted.
> >
> > Regarding the correspondence dated the 28th, the writer notes from perusal of the same that your comments surrounding the reduction in the bill are not acceptable in regard to the alleged errors made and the indication given by the writer to yourself surrounding the costs of the matter.
> >
> > The writer takes this opportunity to confirm the telephone message left on your answering machine regarding the outstanding bill and the reduction of the same in that a further reduction in the sum of £500 plus VAT off our profit costs would be the final figure upon which we are able to reduce the said amount.
> >
> > Please find enclosed copy sealed Order for your retention.
> > We will advise you of taxation in due course.
>
> Few clients receiving this letter would feel that their affairs were in the hands of the sharpest thinker in the West. And I reckon few lawyers, whether traditional or modern in their drafting, would regard it as anything but grotesque and unacceptable. Yet some writers seem to feel that their passport to the profession will only remain valid if they drench

> their writing with similar legal flavouring – words like *hereinafter, said, aforesaid, notwithstanding* and *herein*, together with those three ugly sisters *thereof, whereof* and *hereof*. None of these is a term of art; all are alien to most clients' normal speech and writing and can be removed or replaced with everyday English. Lawyers who really take their writing seriously would even delete the ubiquitous *Please find enclosed* in favour of *I enclose*; few envelopes are so huge that clients have to send in a search party and *find* the contents.
>
> (Cutts, 1991, pp. 40–1)

What was your view of David O'Brien's reaction to this way of altering workplace use of English, as explained on this band? Remember that Martin Cutts is approaching the issue partly from the general public's viewpoint, while David O'Brien considers what he sees as the needs of the company and its management. It is interesting that they both used a similar term in talking about what they disapproved of; Martin Cutts spoke of a 'foggy style' while David O'Brien chose the opposite approach to avoid 'fuzziness'. Is this one of the problems of trying to talk about language?

Band 8 Work talk

(Duration: 3 minutes; study time: about 45 minutes)

Before listening

This band is intended to give you further practice at transcribing spoken English, as well as drawing together your ideas on the use of English at work.

The band contains an extract from a simulation exercise in a training programme, in which a panel of interviewers discuss the merits of two candidates for a job, whom they have just interviewed. We suggest that you listen carefully to the tape a couple of times.

Next, try making a rough transcript of the discussion, using either a 'standard' or 'column' transcript. To do this you will have to look back through section 6.4 of *Describing Language*, or any notes you made on this chapter, and decide which layout you would prefer for this kind of discussion. You should now try out some brief analyses of this extract of talk, relating this to points made in the course book, Chapter 3. We suggest you look through your transcript and replay the band as necessary, in order to make brief notes on:

- how the group is using English to achieve their set goal of agreeing on the best person for the job;
- any evidence that they are operating as a discourse community;
- how they cooperate on deciding what they are looking for and how they support each other in shaping the decision;
- whether one participant takes some control in bringing the group's views together; look at the function of questions within the group, and how they are answered;
- any use of implicit references to their shared experience in this field of work;
- any work-related jargon.

This analysis would provide an interesting comparison with your study of the informal discussion between Pip and Phyllis at the end of week 10. You could also think about how this group's discussion relates to any similar group discussion you may have taken part in recently, at work, in a tutorial or in a leisure activity, when you have tried to reach an agreed decision.

Band 9 Rhetoric and persuasion

Contributors: *Sarojini Naidu,* an Indian politician, feminist and poet; *C. Kuykendall,* an American educationist

(Duration: 7 minutes; study time: about 40 minutes)

Sarojini Naidu (Popperfoto)

Before listening

Listening to this band will help you to review the ideas and language styles discussed in week 13. It contains two examples of rhetoric for you to listen to and analyse.

Sarojini Naidu (1879–1949) was an Indian politician, feminist and poet. She was active in the Indian independence movement and was sentenced to prison several times in the 1930s and 1940s. She was the first woman to be appointed president of the National Congress (in 1925). After independence in 1947 she became governor of the United Provinces (now Uttar Pradesh). The speech you hear on Band 9 was made to a large crowd around the time of independence.

The second recording is from an American educationist, C. Kuykendall, addressing a crowded meeting in New Orleans.

If your interest in transcribing is developing, you may like to gain further practice by transcribing short sections of each speech. You will find the list of transcription symbols in the Appendix to Chapter 4 of the course book useful, especially the way of representing frequency and length of applause.

If not, listen carefully a couple of times. As you listen to the first speaker, jot down notes on these points:

- What signals are her audience picking up to indicate that it is the right time to applaud?
- What rhetorical device is she using to get her message across?

While listening to the second speaker, you will be aware of her use of the stylistic feature of 'call and response'. Here she is helping the audience, some of whom are not familiar with this cultural tradition, to take part by giving them interactive roles to play. Listen for examples of this; note down the audience's responses and what devices and points in her speech trigger them off. Also note any other rhetorical devices she uses to gain her effects.

VIDEO

Producer: *Anne Diack*

Academic consultant for Bands 2 and 3: *Neil Mercer*

Band 2 English at work

(Duration $5\frac{1}{2}$ minutes; study time: about 45 minutes)

Before viewing

This band is part of week 12 and accompanies Chapter 3 of the course book.

The band contains two short extracts for you to analyse. They show specific uses of English in the workplace. Both take place in the office of an estate agent in Milton Keynes, in the south of England, which specializes in selling houses in the northern part of the town and surrounding areas. The two estate agents who appear in the extract are members of this firm's staff. The client in the first extract is a postgraduate student at the Open University; she lives in a house similar to the one that she describes, although there have been minor changes to the exact details of its location, to preserve her privacy. The second of the two extracts shows an incident that occurred as part of the normal business of this firm, on the day that filming took place.

You will quickly realize that these extracts show different aspects of the use of English in the working situation. In businesses such as this, language is used in one way in dealing with customers and in another between colleagues, to organize and plan their activities. You will recall the discussion of this in Chapter 3; but there is relevant material elsewhere. We list below the sources you can turn to to help you analyse this band.

We would now like you to use these two extracts for your own analysis of the ways in which English is used in the workplace. Compare and contrast the use of English in each extract, with particular emphasis on the different purposes the conversations seem to fulfil in each case and the linguistic features that help to achieve these purposes.

Watch the extracts at least once through to get a general sense of each discussion. Then decide on what each speaker seems to be trying to achieve as they talk and watch each extract more carefully, stopping the tape where necessary to note down significant words or phrases that contribute to the aims and purposes of the speakers. Features to look out for include:

- The content of each conversation; does this in itself mark out one conversation as being between colleagues and another as being between client and professional?
- The use of technical terms and specialist jargon – does this vary between the conversations? If so, why? (It doesn't matter if you don't understand all the jargon, unless you actually are an estate agent!)
- How far the speakers feel the need to be explicit in what they say; how far they can assume prior knowledge – this is more obvious in the second extract, but consider also how much shared knowledge of the Milton Keynes area the first two speakers have.
- The use of questions and other devices to obtain information, and the purposes of obtaining that information.
- Sentence structure – are all utterances complete statements? How far do the speakers support and complement each other, and what linguistic devices do they use to do so? Are there any special phrases for opening or closing the conversation or for changing the topic?
- The tone of each speaker; the use of non-verbal means such as gestures, posture and gaze, and what they contribute to the overall effect.

Also list any other features that you notice.

Then you can draw up an overall comparison, looking for similarities and differences between the conversations, related to their different purposes and setting within a particular workplace. To help you, refer back to the following sources (especially the sections of Chapter 3):

- course book Chapter 3, sections 3.1, 3.2, 3.3 and Readings A and B.
- course book Chapter 1, sections 1.1 and 1.2;
- the material on Halliday's theories that you collected together in week 12;
- Audiocassette 3 Band 5, in which you considered the techniques of conversational support used by Pip and Phyllis;
- Audiocassette 3 Band 7, where speakers discuss jargon in the workplace;
- Audiocassette 3 Band 8 and the work you did on its example of language used for a particular work-related purpose by the interview panel.

Band 3 Public speaking

(Duration: 4½ minutes; study time: about 45 minutes)

Before viewing

This band should help you review your work in week 13, and also prepare for Block 4, *English as art.*

The band contains three extracts from the speeches of well-known public speakers for you to study and analyse for yourself. In some ways it is easier to study rhetoric in this way, as it is essentially a performance art in which the non-verbal elements combine with the words and their associations to create the desired impact on the hearer. (We shall be discussing language as a performance art in more detail in Block 4.)

We have chosen speakers who had considerable influence in their own countries and also across the world.

Mrs Margaret Thatcher, British Conservative politician (now Baroness Thatcher); born in Grantham, England, in 1925; daughter of a local politician and Methodist lay preacher; leader of the Conservative party from 1975 to 1990 and first woman prime minister of Great Britain from 1979 to 1990.

Martin Luther King, American civil rights leader; born in Atlanta, Georgia, USA, in 1929; son of a Baptist minister. He followed his father into the church and became a minister in Alabama, one of the southern states of the USA; became a leader of the civil rights movement in America in the 1960s, working for equal rights for black Americans; assassinated in Memphis, Tennessee in 1968.

Nelson Mandela, South African civil rights leader and politician; born in the Transkei in 1918; early leader of the African National Congress, campaigning for rights for black South Africans; imprisoned for political activity in 1964; released in 1990; became first black president of the Republic of South Africa in 1994.

These three speakers have different intentions in making their speeches and there are obvious differences in their rhetorical styles. However, they all share the aim of persuading their hearers to share their point of view, and to make them willing to take some form of action as a result of listening to them.

Use these three extracts to analyse the speakers' use of rhetorical devices to convey their message and gain an effect on their audience. First, using the brief biographical details given above, jot down what you think each speaker will be aiming to persuade their hearers to believe. Watch and listen to the three extracts once, to get an overall impression of what the speakers are saying. Then undertake a more detailed analysis. Play the tape again several times, stopping the tape after each speaker and during the extracts when necessary. During these viewings, make notes on these features, and on any others that occur to you:

- the words and phrases that are given the greatest importance; the use of emotive vocabulary; the use of repetition;
- the use of rhetorical devices, such as three-part lists and contrasts;
- the ways in which the speaker signals to the audience that an important point has been made, and that they should respond;
- the use of any significant pauses, and the contexts in which they occur;
- the use of inflections of the voice and changes of tone.

Also note down any other features of their rhetorical style that you think of as you watch and listen.

Now we would like you to concentrate on the non-verbal components which give support to the words of the speech. Play the extracts again, but *without* watching; just listen to the speakers' words. Then replay them, but this time watch carefully for the use of non-verbal features like gesture, gaze and posture. Think how these are used to emphasize and underline the words and their significance, and to help in creating audience response.

Now draw up a comparison of the rhetorical techniques used by the three speakers. Consider whether, and how far, they are influenced by any of the rhetorical traditions that have been discussed in Chapter 4. There are some interesting points to consider here – for instance, can we talk of a black or African tradition of which both Martin Luther King and Nelson Mandela are equally representative? Does King's style relate more closely to the tradition of church preaching in which he grew up and was trained? Are there any noticeable similarities between the techniques of the two politicians, despite their different origins and views? Are there any traces of the sermons of Margaret Thatcher's British Methodist upbringing in her rhetorical style? If so, does it differ from King's style, influenced by the preaching style of the southern USA? Where do these speeches fit into the cultural expectations of their hearers? How much response, and of what kind, does each speaker expect, and how is this signalled to the audience?

These, and other points, will probably occur to you as you watch and think about the extracts.

You will also find it useful to compare these extracts with those on Audiocassette 3 Band 9. How do the styles of rhetoric in the extracts on video relate to these? What similarities and differences do you notice? Is there a difference in impact between a speech that you only hear and one that you can both see and hear? If you have audio or video recordings of any other speaker using English to make a public speech, or if you have the opportunity to watch a speaker, live or on TV, making a speech or giving a religious address, it would be interesting to use this as a further comparative investigation into rhetorical styles in different contexts and cultures. You can also listen critically to people's participation in meetings such as local pressure groups, societies and political movements.

REFERENCES

CUTTS, M. (1991) 'Clear writing for lawyers. Advice by a Plain English campaigner to writers of legalese' in *English Today*, no. 25, January, pp. 40–1.

JOHNSON, T.H. (ed.) (1960) *The Complete Poems of Emily Dickinson,* Boston, Little Brown.